Fossilized Dendrites
from Mars

Poems

Davanna Cimino

Several of the poems in this volume were published in *Poems from the Beach and Other Places*, 2019.

Formatted with Vellum

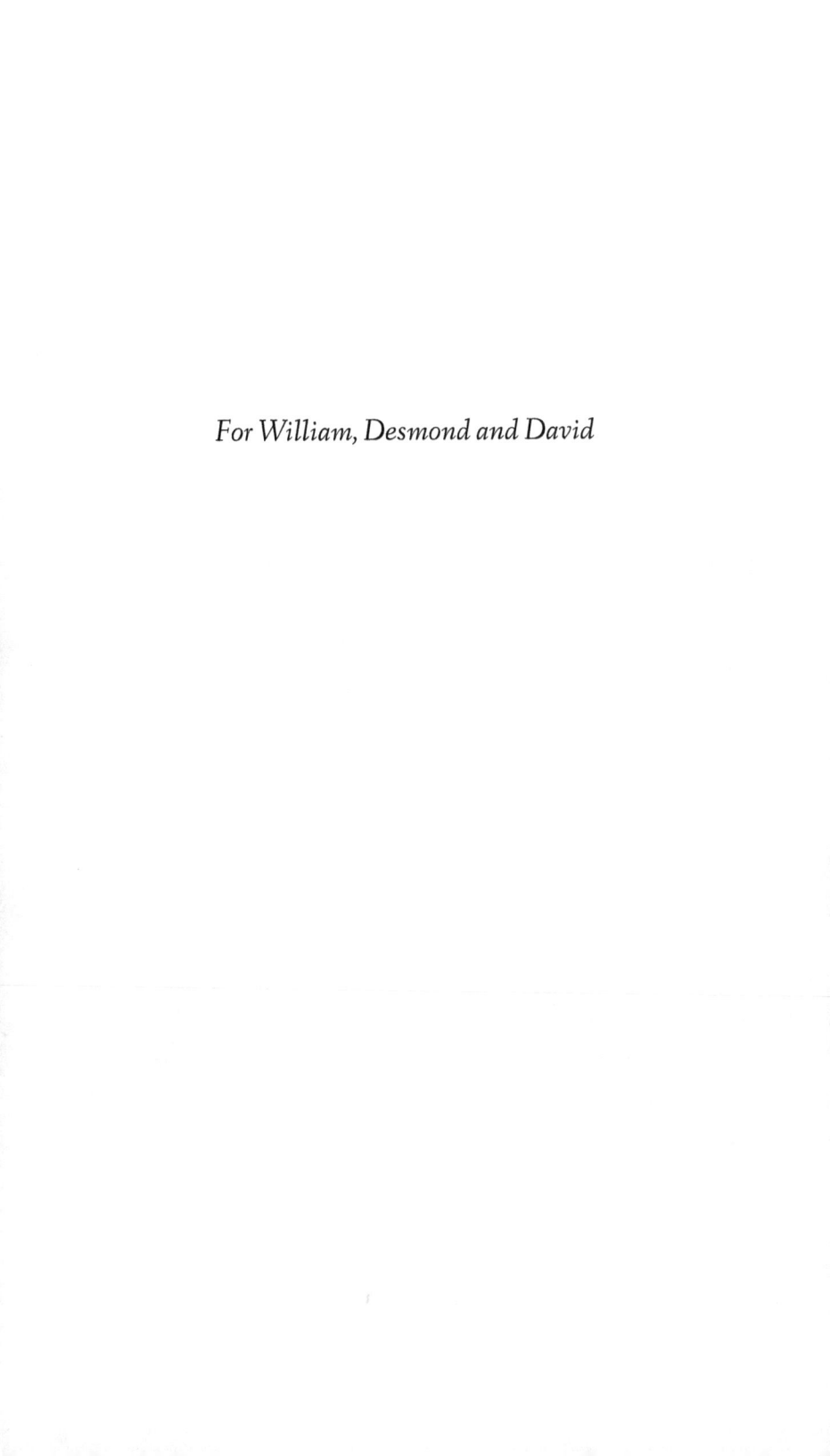

For William, Desmond and David

Contents

Plague

Fossilized Dendrites from Mars

It was raining yesterday when you came.
I always feel the need to protect you.
You're as vulnerable as a child.
You with your heart-edged communist manifesto
that I can never understand.
Bird song and raptor cry sound like knells
from another realm.
One without our DNA but into which we can see.

This is where the magic comes.

This is where reason cannot go.
Reason can only take you so far.
The rest is love. And you can't know it.
You have to let it take you.
That's very hard to arrange.

It's like slipping off a rock into a foamy, heaving sea
that gestures in muscular waves to the jagged cliffs.
But there are caves in the cliffs, if you can get there.
Caves where Cheddar Man and
Neanderthals wait out eternity.

The seagull's cry punctuates the air
full of molecules of salt, of moss, of quartz, of moon dust.
Sun-baked seaweed.
Sun and surf scour wood.
Calcium carbonate.
Plankton, shrimp, exoskeletons.
Fossilized dendrites from Mars.

Diatoms.

Diatomaceous earth.
Regenerative splurge.
"In my world one diatom is worth one thousand of you."
And, "In my world, we don't correct anything", said the
ornery mage. "If you died and came to me, you could be
my queen."

Was this a metaphorical death? I wonder hopefully.

That's me, Charlie Girl*, talking to my nonexistent
conjured-up conjurer, Bryshear*.
He looks a bit like Richard Harris singing "MacArthur
Park" before his Dumbledore days.

He's a Lightning Celt, the likes of which
decorated Europe (prefiguring chivalry by millennia)
in the shadows of prehistory.

Herodotus could only remember the Celt.

The Celt sought no legacy.

*characters in a novel

Viernes Santo (April 10, 2020)

This world is so polluted.
So deluded.
Into which reason has intruded,
and the forests of time, denuded.

Listen to Pontus.
He's trying to breathe
under the heaving seas.
He drowns in pathos
and unspent love.

In the paradise of sea and sky
on St. Joseph Sound
the wavelets thunder softly
against the sea wall.
Listen. Gulping. Listen.

At 3 p.m., Viernes Santo.
No one listens.

Yet I hear the man's voice
tumbling through the sea grapes.

Worried and worried about
what may happen in the financial paralysis.
Throwing out numbers and dollar signs.
Just thinking out loud.

His voice is like a baby's
who still needs his mother's breast
but can't find it—
and so will starve to death.

He shouts amounts
into the pane attached
to his brain.

An obscure, small motor
whines in the distance
across the Sound
where only the fish belong.
And the birds.
The young osprey
sets out to find a meal
with the utmost confidence that he will.

If he can't he will lay down
under the pine tree
on the white beach and die.

A dolphin's fin cuts the surface
rolling on the lapping wavelets.
It's a sign—
the lone dolphin,
the holy priest.
Traveling alone
through space that has no limits.

Torquemada comes
with the religion of men.
And the conquest,
the barren conquest,
yields ashes and ropes of ashes.

And unnatural pigments unconscious of love.

Hipponoe's Horses

Meet me on the spoil island.

Under the starry sky.

Where white-maned Hipponoe's horses
charge light-footedly along the shore.

Hipponoe's Horses
in loose formation,
mouths foaming—
pass through the gateway
to the Sea of Nevermore.
Hora fugit.
Why do you fight it?

Meet me on the island, my love
for it will soon disappear under the waves.

Listen to the blue, metallic craik of the tern,
And to the wind whistling through the rigging
of ships that sail at dawn.

There'll be no one left,
when the seabird bare perches
high on the stretch of Hyperion's vault.
Where we all go to die.

The wind-dessicated carcass
is all that's left on the sand,
where you left your love alone
to follow the ways of man.

If the keening osprey calls you
follow him—
follow him down
to Hipponoe's salty berth
beneath the waves.
Below the well-lit town.

Her horses will take you.
Ride them there
from the shore to the deep.

To a limestone cave
beneath the green, lulling sea.

Come away, come away
Come away down.
Wearing your seaweed crown.

The wilds of the deep
your secret will keep.

In silence the pelican glides overhead.
Its shadow kisses the ground.
God's island is on fire—
those who praise him
watch it burn.

Ignoring their desire.
Contemptus mundi.
Spurn.
In an effort to be holy
you defile our common throne.
Walking in the steps of Jesus—
but He walks alone.

Love in the Time of Pestilence

For the sake of argument
let's just say I love you.
And let's just say that
I have been in love with you
for a long time.
Even though I never see you.
We never talk.

And let's say I can't forget you—
Across years filled with
grief, hunger, anger, joy,
despair and hope.
Across years without you.
You never left my heart.
Even though I barricaded it
from the outside, you were already there.

And even though I tried to smoke you out,
you thrive on holy smoke.

And even though I have lived lifetimes without you,
forging new karma in Prometheus' fire.

It's astonishing to note,
and let's just say for the sake of argument
that the love endured and was nourished by
the ash and smoke from the sacred fire.

Petals rain down from flowers
that always surround me.
Alone, at last.
And still in love.

Even the resting butterfly
reminded me with the colored signal of its wings.
And the cardinal found the highest pylon
from which to proclaim itself king of birds.
Full of song that travels far,
when all the world stops
in this time of crowned pestilence.

Trailing Eos bringing light from the eastern sky,
is a figure on a pale horse.

The accompanying silence forces me to consider
the reality of you
and the way I still love you.

It took the horseman
to bring back to me.
You.

Milk Sky Island/Plague, Day Thirty

Don't trouble me down
with your sudden, trite staircase.
Verbiage drown.

Burble water words,
worlds apart day.
Under similar clouds
tufting into space.

Nurse's lunch
on the bench
takes prominence.

Nut-brown crone.
Suited, Lana Turner-style.
Ready to take possession.
Ready to claim the territory

in the name of the crown of heaven.
Arms akimbo, feet planted in horse stance
on the seawall, mighty.

But whose heaven
above the milky vault?

Loquacious fishermen
compare notes about the virus.
Cast their jovial nets
and bait the hook
for snook.

Boats motoring
on the intracoastal
behind the uninhabited islands
fight back the birds.

This is my territory
and I lay claim to all creation,
in your name, jealous demigod.

Pulling strings
you answer to no one.

The Inquisition of the Surf

A line of sails on the horizon winking a signal.
I forgot to realize that was beautiful.

Conversos.
Moriscos.
Conquistadores.
Ended up on these shores.
How does such a thing happen?

The sane willet stood questioning the surf.
When I entered the undertow dragged at my legs.
I thought of swimming to Cuba.
With the old Conversos, Moriscos and Conquistadores.

The sails that happened to be there winked,
blinding on the day of the solar eclipse.
Where is love on the surface of the sun?

Why look for it there?
It doesn't matter.

The old willet elegantly picked his way along the surf.
Somewhere in my life, there used to be you.
Somewhere on the surface of the sun
my heart ran out of love.
Somewhere underwater, a cormorant swims.
He's a lucky bird—swimming, floating, flying
according to his whim.

The surf comes in frequent, pulsing waves
groaning softly and a little madly as they pattern a song.
The surf questions me, but I can't listen.
The sound makes no reference to my heart.

My heart has left me on the strand alone.
In my pocket, a sea-worn stone.
To swim far—
to Cuba?
With a cormorant as companion, and the sane willet.
Everything that happens here has happened before,
he seemed to imply.

The surf will never tell you why.

It only asks.

Death

The desert is not nostalgic
The rain trails downward,
slight ribbons of lead.

Memories pulverized into sand.
Spider's dream spun dross.
Shadows of indignant crows.
Murderous birds in rows of thorn
shine out of the sun.

The desert is not nostalgic.
It is silent in the face of eternity.
(Only the ocean speaks to the sky.)
Sky burial vultures fly into the high desert.
Broad wings beat thin air,
seethe heavy bodies heavenward
in a sea of light.

Birds, Nature and God

In Cicada Year

In cicada year.
In a forest dense with emotion,
the clouds stream before the hurricane.
The trees and everyone knew,
but I forgot to tell you:
The information in my palm.
The information in a bird's wing.
I heard the cicada sing.

Tricolored heron like a little tin soldier
makes his way across the sky alone.
(Herons are always alone, unlike gulls.
The lazy gulls never work for food.)

The round of the cicada buzzes from tree to tree
like the coconut telegraph.
Code unknown.

If you could decipher the *zeezy-bzz*
you might know enough to win the lottery.

That year, the year the cicada dug itself out of the
blue-gray sand licked with the tannin-stained rain,
and climbed up the rough bark after bursting forth
from the nymph capsule.
It left its shell for some kid to find.
And flew away on 3D-printed wings.

The ultra-bass from the hood
and the mockingbird woodsong—trilling, thrilling.
Then one last angry percussive buzz and rest.
And more trumble from the thundercloud,
low forerunner of storms.

The cicada's body makes a dim noise
like an alien spacecraft
of which there are plenty.
The mockingbird makes it last rounds
from the clothesline to branch,
to nowhere before dark.

Yellow-Crowned Night Heron

Underneath dark heaven.
Stalking mud flats, mud.
Crushing nothing ether

Bubbles in the blood.

Fiddler crab's eye stalks flatten down.

The baleful amber gaze
points the piercing vice-beak,
as swivels slowly the bright-plume head.

Splayed wings warn.
Wickedness has its way while goodness sleeps.

Infrared vision seeks signature pilled-sand retreat.
Scurry and reach.
Escape the beak,
and the fluttering,
pointy plume.
Precise-stepped,
careful bird advances.

Shadow announces doom.

The Last Pelican

Down that sea path, parched.
Shedding heat.
Cooling iridescence in the clouds
takes my mind to ice crystals.

Why is my love an angel?
I can't reach up there.

His heart is tender.
His life is the strong call of a curlew.

Lonely bird.
He seems to be the symmetry of light.

Down that sea path,
parched.

Remembering prickly pear,
and a black snake there,
looking for a fix.

The subtle sky so passive
breaks your heart with beauty.

The effort of a jet leaves a shining trail.
An announcement wrong, yet beautiful
in its futility of flight.

Rain shadow curtain meets the sea
at the horizon
below the rose altostratus and the silver cirrus.
Beaming and fading.
No intention.

The trajectory of the jet glows.
The purplish shroud enfolds,
obscuring its attempt at art.

The sun goes down,
leaving in its wake
pillows of glowing mammatus,
a purple dragon,
and a cossack's hat.

The sky darkens here,
brightens there.
Arriving wind.
Taught colors—
aquamarine,
rose lilac,
sea mist green.

One last pelican glides away on a blade of air.

The curlew's keening note
follows the sun around the sea.
The sea threatening to flood the
barque of my heart with unwanted rest.

The angel of love
is away and eternal—
taking an hibiscus flower to his ear.

Putting the oil of the rose on a shell.
Preparing God's winding-sheet.

Little Blue Heron

Little blue heron
befuddled in
gray metallic sky.

Hot winds heating up
from the furnace where
the atmosphere is thinnest
against the sun.

An hour from death,
what will you do?
An hour from death,
I think only of you.
An hour from death,
I am glad to go.
An hour from death,
to a place I won't know.

To a God not expecting me,
for I seldom prayed.
My own desires
my only ways.
My own cares
my sole concern.
My own love
my triumphant tragedy.

A love I could never have.
A love succored in God's glory.
But the splendor soon forgotten
a moment after leaving the sanctuary.
Forgetting the tabernacle I had become
only so briefly—
before the flood of
information on the superhighway of strife,
overwhelmed divine oneness,
overwhelmed the sanctified life.

The little blue heron
balletic, ungainly, flies in heat.
Looking for a marsh.
Finding only street.

And on the blacktop I wince against the sun.
And pray for you, my love.
I pray for you.

Birds Flew Up

Her heart turned to birds
when she heard him singing.

The birds dispersed
and flew up into the ether—
to roost in lower nirvana.

Think, as Clouds

Think, as clouds march 'round
the ever-turning orb we live upon.
At night, the tenderest vapor ground.
The solid sky. The light-limned sound.
The sea exhaling brine-breath
blown over land communicates along the sand
a xylophonic ripple to the air.
Below the pink-tinged drift I sit.

In the night, a sad liturgy a solemn priest intones.
Practicing his rituals alone.
If not he, then who would take up this wearying task?
The faces of the clouds yet ask.

The host that envelops the world
is from this solitary benediction unfurled.

The priest's orisons rise slow and curled.
As smoke from the thurible upward glowing,
and pearled like dew upon serene grass.
Lodged in souls and forever entwined
within the hearts of a mankind.

Day into Night

Mary's robe enfolds the sky, blue.
Iridescent fish scale clouds form beyond the palm fronds,
breezing, whispering love.

The invisible moon waning gibbous, love.
The cardinal's rich chirrup, love.
The floating jasmine scent, love.
The perfect air, love.
The warm communion of the
eye-of-God sun.
Love.

Signifying night,
the crickets minting coins of gold
to throw into the purple-drift night sky
endlessly chime
one God-haunted note.

Upward, the ringing sword of cricket song
cleaves the tobacco blue
forest of clouds.

If I followed the tidal stream to its source (an old spring)
there I would find a genius centered in the world's amnion,
pulsing slowly with heat and sorrow.

My heart's vault that was empty
fills with leaves and wine and salt.

Under the eternity of Mary's blue robe
my love waits.

Mistaken Love

I Thought I Knew You

I thought I knew you
but there was nothing to know but an echo.
Nothing to see but a mirror reflection.
No words to hear but borrowed charm.
Stolen from some heart less leaden.

Your well-crafted mask
meant to deaden
the blast of unfelt pain.
Unclaimed.

Love's call forbidden,
corralled and ridden
like a spirited horse.

St. Augustine

I wanna go back to Saint Augustine.
I wanna see the green fish fly.
I wanna see your face across the inlet
where I never swam.

In my dreams, I found places
amid shadows and traces—
shorebirds nodding,
tall ships in squalls.
Swells smash on cliffs.
Dark monastery walls.

In a foreign library dream a lone figure walks on the heath.
In city daylight, a small church shines.
Martyrs tombs sing underneath.
Old hymns comfort the sinning saints.
Pop music bleats modern complaints.

In this land where Druids roamed,
I thought I had found a home.

What is the sin that must be expiated by so much waiting?

The waters, the waters know.
I told you so, I told you so.

I wanna go back to Saint Augustine.
To night fishing on a pier,
watching sea turtles roam 'round,
breathe and disappear.

On the pier, a man in black stands
with his back to me.
In his vest, a holy relic allows no conversation.

The relic belongs to the sea.
The sea that took him from me.
The waves bring him back, and away.
Ever and anon I pray,
bring him back to stay.

The prayer remains on the strand.
The relic in my hand.

Druid Moon

The upturned horns of the hazy
Druid moon crown
caught in the crook of the oak tree's trunk,
drift down into
the deep green sea,
nearly black.

Drifting down—now pinking.
My Druid—what were you thinking?
To have put off your crown.
I see it sinking
into the greeny sea.

(What you feared was a
a Catholic schoolgirl.
Only me.)

I could never pluck the halo
from your golden head.
You had only to bow to the deep
and it fell, instead—
sliding into the Gulf,
blood red.

And there its
sorrow will keep.

What the Christian fears
is what the Druid knows—
that there is no sin, but blame.

For God would not
condemn to hell
the soul containing the flame.

The furnace of stars dwells
within us all.
We never have been
nor will we ever be
in Satan's thrall.
It's the penumbra of
our shadow cast out
that benights our puny minds with doubt.

So lift up your head
and recognize
the glory of God
before your eyes.

The murmuring dark sea, heaving
reaches up,
breathing.
To join heaven.
A part of itself.
Leaving,
Then cleaving.

Leaving,
cleaving.

I Hearted a Crusader

I hearted a crusader once.
He loved only Jerusalem.

Jerusalem, Jerusalem.

Was the Holy Lamb of God
ever in this fickle heart seen?
Was not Jerusalem builded here
amid dark, satanic desire?

The earthly clods are at odds
with the cathedral's insistent spire.

God-installed desire—a passage to the fire.
Announces the solitary bell.
Tolling the heart's death knell.
Whirlwind-heated destination—

the second circle of hell.

Against this fate, the crusader walled his heart
in a whitened tomb.

And none shall know, but the shades,
the love buried in the ruin.

The Hissing Foam

The hissing foam of the
high surf rears up on waves
large enough to drown in.
(I am lonely for you.)

In the breakers' roar and tumult upon the shore
a question forms:

Where is your love?

I answer that my love is a sailor
with a golden halo and a heart made of
oceans' tears and petals and fire.

His strength is as continuous as
the beat of the petrel's wing as it soars
across the world on the wind of light.

His love is anchored in seaweed beds
that float upon the celestial sea
trailing phosphorescently tinted wakes.
When he alights upon land
he leaves glowing footprints in the sand.

His soul flies on the solar wind—
not meaning to be careless
but not caring where it goes.

He will come back in a wooden boat.
To find me waiting here,
thumbing notebooks filled with poems
written in squid ink
by a sea witch who mocks me.
And collecting driftwood
to burn in my hearth.

He might laugh at me then,
for being so absorbed with trivial tasks.
While he strides across land masses,
collects rings from Saturn,
activates a dead comet,
slides down the crescent moon,
and washes away time.

Girls and children and men and people of all kinds
will feel a slight thrill when he passes them in their
dreams.

The Bottom of the Heart

At the bottom of the heart
a song of whales begins.
Sounding the depths in underwater caverns,
the cosmic wind rushes in
the door left open.

The breath of earth, a love song played—
the death of the heart, a long, slow fade.

The door at the bottom of the heart
left open for you is closing now.
The sun's shine sea spray
once revealed the entryway.
Now it's just another passion play.
Life goes on.
As always.

I'll Tell You

I'll tell you how to bear unwanted love.
Bear it lightly on your shoulder,
like the dove of the Holy Spirit—
only not holy, just worldly.
A worldly song, which even in its homeliness
can show you the way to heaven
if you haven't already gotten there,
or ever doubted its existence.

I don't understand the cries of birds
as they dart through the air.
The knowing cries of birds
untie the skeleton of love,
drying tears, freshening blood.

Dry sinews and ribbons of flesh
decorate the wren's nest.

Fibers from a frond not burnt
to smudge the foreheads of the faithful
and remind them
unto dust.
Fibers from the frond
lining the wrens' nest,
which they abandon
to build another
in an uninhabited place.

The lived-in heart
cannot accommodate birdsong.
The rush of blood is too loud,
and drowns out the song
in a cataract swollen with tears.

Creatures, Dreams and Letters

Nostalgia, for Spain

I feel it coming on a strange landscape edging towards me
like Salvador Dalí. A plateau in the distance, kissed by
zephyrs and creamy light.

Is it possible to forestall its arrival?

The globe is big, but this ocean is wider,
and intersects with Dalí's home.

Insects, flying knives, knaves and astronauts live there.

And the prince of Old Spain,
Who long ago laid down under murmuring cypress trees.
His breath expressed silver mirrors to the moon
burnt black by the prayers of a tortured saint.

I Am Not Caliban

I live inside a
beached whale
where it is sure to be
rather salt.
You say I broke your heart.

It's not my fault.
I am not Caliban.

I am not Caliban.
You are.
A monster on a
rocky beach.
Who spoils the place for man.

I am not Caliban.
You are.

A creature who eats
kelp for breakfast—
that the crabs won't have.
The crab is a singer
more special than you.
That's me.
A sea mite
on the back of a whale.

Singing permanently,
and whole.

Pescaditos

The tiny fish,
pescaditos,
swim as one under
the surface of the water.

The mute fish
evading and consuming
one another.

The fish disappears willingly into
the gullet of a needle fish.
The minnow's scales glimmer—
fine, sparkling particles
profusing the atmosphere with surrender.

Terrestrial path
past the high school.

Pre-formed, never to be fully-matured adults
projectile vomiting
monosyllabic cries of "fuck"
into the exhaust-filled air.
Toxins emitted by their luxury vehicles.

If, in their pornography-informed embrace,
a child is conceived,
there is killing technology available for a price.
Very small.
No consequences need attach.
Inured to flat groping, starless stares,
we hope for nothing.
And are satisfied.

On asphalt.
a spread fan of plumage.
The corpus' energy expended in evading
motors of blowers and mowers
lies smashed on the black.
The eye open to the sky holds an expression of fear.

Lorca's grave is hidden in Old Spain.
That world, gone now,
Was visited by satyrs, drinking horses
and dusty mourning doves.
Existent chimeras? Daily occurrences.
And sunflowers.

Technology is merely on or off.
The light is artificial. The colors are simulated.
Notice the insistent sun pounding in a glazed-blue sky.
Coronal mass ejection.

Fact: the explosion on the surface of the ovum
is when the life begins.

The Creature from the Black Lagoon (Part One)

I never realized before that I have webbed fingers.
How could such a thing have escaped my notice?
you might ask.

Perhaps it's the fact that I'm in my fifties now.
The skin on my hands is loose and tanned—
so the webbing shows as pale tissue in the cleft
between my fingers as I spread them.
Perhaps it's not even true webbing.
Perhaps it's only my aging skin.

Yet, I prefer to think that my fingers and toes are webbed.
That way I'm more like
the Creature from the Black Lagoon—
a lonely, murderous beast
who lived in the beautiful Silver River
in North Central Florida, near where I was born.

I have so much in common with this reptilian outcast.
We are both lonely. We both love water.
We are both great swimmers,
and I can see well in the dark.
I swim underwater with balletic strokes—
like the creature.
I admire his secretive, observant nature.
He, like me, is aware of any intruder
into his watery paradise.
He kills his foes.

I merely despise mine.

An Official-Sounding Letter

I wrote you an official-sounding letter.
I first trimmed it of emotion.
And subtracted the scent of roses
I had rubbed into the crease of the paper
which I wanted to kiss.

All that was left was some efficient words.
And no birdsong.

The whole world stopped and wept.
Memories fled.
A tangled mass of neurons bled tar into the brain.

This is the result of my official-sounding letter.

God, I Pray the Atheists Are Right

Now, the wait
for the end of time.
Or my time, at least.
At which time I will cease to exist.
And so will this deep ache.

Unless the Buddhists are correct,
and I am reborn
into a similar dilemma,
or worse.
(Maybe I'll be reborn as a snake or something.)

Unless the Christians are right,
and I'll find myself
ensconced in a place
of eternal torment
with all sorts of unspeakable

acts being perpetrated by and upon me.
And me shrieking with a
permanently open mouth
like the demented, depraved
character in Fellini's film.
The one who lives in a cave of cement blocks
on a stretch of deserted beach.
The crazy one called Vulpina.

God, I pray the atheists are right.
Because I just want it to end.
Although, thinking stoically,
it could always be worse.
I could be missing four limbs,

and my head.

I will muddle through, somehow.

* *Self pity*, home remedies for:
Dutch courage, Mrs. Miniver, arranging deck chairs,
gallows humor, Morrissey.

Erica Kane's Fiasco

I told you what every soap opera queen
lays down in ultimate fashion.
Botoxed.
Trout-lipped
and moneyed.
"I never want to see *YOU*, or talk to *YOU* again!"

Across the eons,
the seas,
the cricket-eternity chime.
Powering the world with Godsong,
but no discourse among equals.

I thought you were a holy man.
My own personal shaman.
A druid. A wizard.

Emerging from the center of the oak.
White-armed. Tender.

(At this point I revert to soap opera histrionics because it
worked so well for Erica Kane.)

"How dare you treat me like that!
Don't you know what I've been through?
And all *FOR YOU!*"

I told you—and I could write with pride—
of love that hurt me.
But no one could see it.

For me, Erica's trick is a failure.
No, I'm only a fool.
A slutty fool, too.

I wanted a man I knew.
I swear I knew.
Many lives ago,
said the Germanic psychic
whose palm I crossed with plastic.
And a timer on the side.
I couldn't think of enough questions to fill
the thirty minutes allotted to my brush with the beyond.
Because I already had consulted my own crystal ball—
witch that I am.

But this is about the man I knew,
I swear I knew.
Many lives ago,
said the psychic.

A monk,
a merchant,
a sailor,
a boy on the strand,
and a saint, now, apparently.
A celibate spy in the house of love.
Provoking passion.
Then extinguishing it with a wink.
Or a kink.
(What is the difference between passion and lust—
have you ever stopped to think?)

He would float if tried for witchcraft.
Whereas I would be sure to sink.
Or maybe it's the other way around.

But a bloody saint now! At least for me whenever I appear.
Me, besmirching everything I behold.
Growing older by the hour.
He, a woman-hating guardian of his own virtue.
Declaiming he must find his keys and shower.

Here under the oaks,
soaked and shining.
I don't dare look.
His beauty is blinding.
He emerges from the trunk.
Fully virile.

Might I make myself innocuous?
Trussed-up in a nun's habit?
Or gussied-up and gormless —
a reality show slut?
Or a suburban poo-bah of recent money
and vacant mind?
As long as I am docile.
That's what's wanted in a modern, female apostle.
Empty-headed, botoxed wonders,
be meek, please, when confronted
with ancient patriarchal blunders.

(I've got a chip on my shoulder
roughly the size of a boulder.)

Here under the oaks.
Me composing. He decomposing.
Me inspecting. He rejecting.
Me versifying.
He absolving—
a far more important function.

He of a noble lineage
from which I am excluded.
One is suitable only if a member
of one's anatomy is extruded into space.

Rather than the obverse
which is worse.

In Strip Malls and Unicorns

I was looking for you.
Then I found you amid such fire.

You felt unsettled,
like unicorns jostling on a dusty plain.

All hemmed-in by hope.
I don't worry about things like license-tags, macadam
motives, transmission fluid, politician's beer.
I prefer not to participate in strip malls.

If you do that, you go to sleep in strip malls.
After an age, you wake up,
and the world is far worse than you remember.

The Idiot Child and the Dog on the Lawn (Wednesday, March 18, 2009)

You are
inside a protective
ranch-style
cement block shelter,
confidently undertaking
home repairs,
With supplies shipped
from warehouses which store mass-produced widgets.

Hence you are able,
under the vault of the
deliriously gorgeous sky—
with clouds arching toward outer space,
in abalone-shell variegations,
and painted in a zillion colors
by You-Know-Who—
to re-grout your bathtub

in the unfractured certitude
that mildew will not mar the
delicious, buttery finish of the silicon goop.

Outside a cloud bursts peach against azure.
A cricket cheers its brethren on with song.
An invisible jet plane roars softly in a straight line
from somewhere west to somewhere east.
Higher up than you can breathe.
And cold, they tell me.

The dog on the lawn, interestedly observing the comings
and goings of the UPS man
delivering his last package of the day,
knows this is all there is.

And the idiot child holds a stuffed red bull in his hand
and revels in his synesthesia.

About the Author

Davanna Cimino lives on the Gulf Coast of Florida. She occasionally writes poetry and is currently working on a novel.

 instagram.com/davannacimino
 x.com/davanna